EARTHQUAKE

Jen Green

W
FRANKLIN WATTS
LONDON • SYDNEY

First published in 2011 by Franklin Watts

Copyright © 2011 Arcturus Publishing Limited

Franklin Watts
338 Euston Road
London NW1 3BH

Franklin Watts Australia
Level 17/207 Kent Street, Sydney, NSW 2000

Produced by Arcturus Publishing Limited,
26/27 Bickels Yard, 151–153 Bermondsey Street, London SE1 3HA

The right of Jen Green to be identified as the author of this work has been asserted by her in accordance with the Copyright, Designs and Patents Act 1988.

All rights reserved.

Series concept: Alex Woolf
Editor and picture researcher: Alex Woolf
Designer: Ian Winton

Picture credits
Corbis: 4 (Peter Turnley), 5 (Lee Celano/Reuters), 6 (Claudio Reyes/epa), 7 (Jorge Silva/Reuters), 8 (Bettmann), 9 (Ted Streshinsky), cover and 11 (Sergio Dorantes/Sygma), 12 (Peter Turnley), 13 (Bernard Bisson/Sygma), 14 (Hyogo Prefectural Government/epa), 15 (Michael S Yamashita), 16 (Xinhua/Sygma), 17 (Xinhua/Sygma), 19 (Lana Slivar/Reuters), 20 (epa), 21 (GEA Search and Rescue team/Handout/Reuters), 22 (Stringer Shanghai/Reuters), 23 (Michael Reynolds/epa), 24 (Eduardo Munoz/Reuters), 25 (IDF/epa), 26 (Kyodo/Xinhua), 27 (STR/epa), 28 (Reuters), 29 (Francis Malasig/epa).

Cover picture: A building collapses following an earthquake in Mexico City in September 1985.

A CIP catalogue record for this book is available from the British Library.

Dewey Decimal Classification Number: 363.3'495

ISBN 978 1 4451 0504 8

Printed in China

Franklin Watts is a division of Hachette Children's Books, an Hachette UK company.
www.hachette.co.uk

Contents

What are Earthquakes?	4
To the Rescue	6
San Francisco, 1906	8
Mexico City, 1985	10
Iran, 1990	12
Kobe, 1995	14
Indonesian Earthquake and Tsunami, 2004	16
Indian Ocean Tsunami, 2004	18
Kashmir, 2005	20
China, 2008	22
Haiti, 2010	24
Japanese Tsunami, 2011	26
Preparing for Earthquakes	28
Glossary	30
Further Information	31
Index	32

What are Earthquakes?

An earthquake is a violent shaking of the ground, caused by rocks shifting deep below the surface. Earthquakes are triggered by the restless movement of the giant rocky plates that form Earth's outer layer. These are called tectonic plates. They ride on the deep layer of red-hot, partly liquid rock below like crusts of bread on a simmering soup.

Faultlines

Most earthquakes strike along deep cracks called faultlines. These mostly lie along boundaries where tectonic plates slowly collide or scrape past each other. Plate movements put tremendous strain on rocks underground. Eventually the rocks shatter and jolt into a new position. Shock waves ripple out from the centre of the quake, called the focus.

In 1988 a major earthquake rocked Armenia in Western Asia, killing thousands of people. Survivors faced freezing winter conditions without shelter.

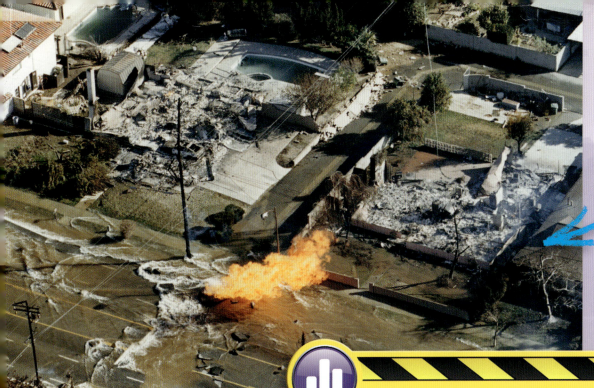

In 1994, a quake in Los Angeles, USA, damaged gas and water pipes. Some streets experienced both floods and fires.

Destructive force

The actual quake lasts only moments. But it can cause huge destruction. The ground heaves and splits open. Hillsides, forests, roads and bridges may be swept away by landslides or avalanches. Whole towns can be flattened, and thousands of people may be killed or trapped by falling buildings.

And that may be just the start of the destruction. All too often, broken gas and electric lines start fires. Rock falls shatter dams, causing floods. Undersea earthquakes can trigger giant waves called tsunamis. Minor quakes, called aftershocks, may continue for weeks as the ground settles.

AT-A-GLANCE

Several scales are used to measure earthquakes. The Richter Scale rates quakes according to their magnitude – strength and intensity. This chart also shows the effects.

Richter magnitudes	Earthquake effects
Less than 2.0	Not felt
2.0–2.9	Generally not felt, but recorded
3.0–3.9	Often felt, but rarely causes damage
4.0–4.9	Furniture shakes, but serious damage unlikely
5.0–5.9	Major damage to poorly constructed buildings over small regions
6.0–6.9	Can be destructive in areas up to 160 km across
7.0–7.9	Can cause serious damage over larger areas
8.0–8.9	Can cause serious damage in areas hundreds of kilometres across
9.0–9.9	Devastating in areas several thousand kilometres across
10.0+	Never recorded

To the Rescue

When an earthquake strikes, sirens wail and emergency services are scrambled. Every second counts when lives are at risk. Roads and railway lines are often damaged, so rescuers usually reach the disaster zone by air. Search and rescue (SAR) teams sift through the ruins for survivors. Sniffer dogs and heat-sensing equipment may be used to locate buried victims. Then rescuers carefully shift the rubble and bring out survivors.

Emergency action

Medical teams treat the injured. Serious cases are rushed to hospital. Meanwhile firefighters tackle fires. The army may be called in to help with the rescue, bury the dead or keep law and order. As news of the disaster spreads, other countries join the relief effort, sending SAR teams, food, supplies and equipment.

Rescue workers and a trained sniffer dog search for survivors in the ruins of a city in Chile after a violent quake in March 2010.

Helping survivors

A major quake may leave tens of thousands of people homeless. Survivors are evacuated to a place of safety. They may be housed in tents or public buildings. Huge quantities of food, clothing and blankets will be needed. Clean water is vital to prevent the spread of disease.

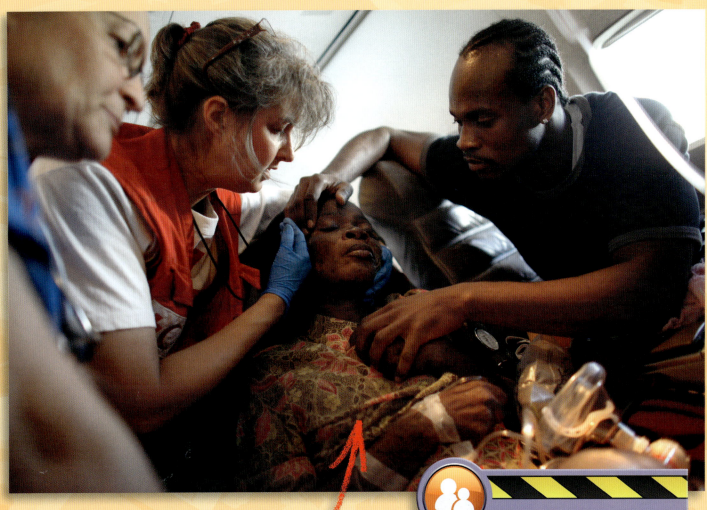

A victim of the 2010 earthquake in Haiti is looked after by her son and a Red Cross worker, while being evacuated.

Reconstruction

In the next weeks and months, bulldozers and cranes clear the rubble. Unsafe buildings are pulled down. Then rebuilding begins. Electricity, gas, water and telephone lines are repaired. Transport links are restored. Eventually schools, shops and health centres reopen, so people can come back if they want to. Normal life returns.

EYEWITNESS

Quake-struck cities are very dangerous places. Rescue teams often risk their own lives to save others. The work is dirty and exhausting. One rescuer in Haiti after the 2010 earthquake (see pages 24–27) said: 'You just keep trying, giving it one hundred per cent, as long as there's any chance of survivors.'

San Francisco, 1906

Dawn, 18 April 1906. All was quiet in the boomtown city of San Francisco. The Pacific-coast town had grown rapidly since gold had been discovered nearby 60 years before. No one knew that the young city was built smack on one of the most dangerous faultlines in the world.

Shaken city

At 5.12 am a violent earthquake rocked the city. Banks, grand hotels and department stores swayed and toppled. An eyewitness reported: 'I heard the crash of falling buildings, the rumble of avalanches of bricks.' Along the shoreline, houses built on loose sand sank and leaned crazily 'like a row of tottering drunks.' People rushed onto the streets in their nightclothes as terrified horses charged past.

This aerial view of central San Francisco shows the devastation caused by the 1906 quake. Buildings that had not been flattened by the shaking were gutted by fire.

Fire!

All over the city, fires were sparked by overturned stoves and gas lamps and live electric wires. Flames leapt from block to block. Firefighters ran out of water because of broken water pipes. People fled with a few possessions or stayed to help the injured. After three days, the fires were finally put out, but two-thirds of the city had burned down. Dazed survivors slept in tents for months.

EYEWITNESS

When water ran out, members of the city's Italian community doused the flames with wine stored in barrels. An eyewitness wrote: 'Barrel heads were smashed in, and the bucket brigade turned from water to wine. Men on the roofs drenched the sides of the house with wine.'

EIGHTY YEARS ON

San Francisco soon rose from the ashes. The city now has one of the strictest building codes in the world. All new buildings are designed to cope with shaking. This helped to reduce the number of deaths when further quakes hit in 1989 and 1994.

The San Francisco quake left around 250,000 people homeless. Survivors spent months in tent cities on open ground, such as public parks.

Mexico City, 1985

In 1985, scientists monitoring an undersea fault off the coast of Mexico noticed that two tectonic plates were pressing against each other. Tension was building up, and an earthquake seemed likely. However, no one guessed that the coming quake would devastate the Mexican capital, 400 kilometres away.

Shock waves

On 19 September 1985, at 7.18 am, a powerful earthquake rocked the seabed. The shaking lasted 20 seconds, triggering landslides in the countryside. In the capital, Mexico City, tall buildings swayed wildly. A 12-storey hotel crashed to the ground, killing 140 people. Mexico's capital had been built on the loose sand of a dried-up lake bed. When the quake struck, the soil vibrated like a drum, increasing the power of the shock waves.

BREAKING NEWS

19 September 1985, Mexico …

A massive earthquake rocked Mexico this morning. The damage is worst in the Mexican capital, home to nearly 19 million people. The city centre has been virtually razed to the ground. Hundreds are believed to be trapped in the ruins.

International rescue

When the shaking stopped, thick smoke and dust filled the air. Rescue workers, soldiers and citizens frantically shifted rubble to free survivors. They were soon joined by rescue teams from North America and Europe, armed with sniffer dogs and detection equipment. However, rescue work stopped when a second massive quake struck the following evening. Aftershocks hindered the recovery in the next weeks and months.

Survivors flee as the Mexico City earthquake brings the multistorey Hotel Regis crashing to the ground. The luxury hotel, built in the early 1900s, was reduced to rubble.

RESCUE!

In Mexico City, the multistorey hospital collapsed like a concertina, killing 600 staff and patients. Amazingly, several newborn babies were lifted unharmed from the rubble up to ten days later. One baby who had been born early had been placed in an incubator, which protected her as the floors above collapsed.

Iran, 1990

The night of 21 June 1990 looked set to be a peaceful one in Gilan Province in north-west Iran. At half-past midnight, most houses were dark. People were either asleep or gathered around flickering TV screens, watching World Cup soccer. Then a violent earthquake shattered the peace.

Landslides

Gilan Province is a mountainous region with settlements in fertile valleys. The earthquake triggered over 400 landslides on steep hillsides. Rockslides buried 700 villages in valleys. In the town of Roudbar, 90 per cent of buildings were destroyed, and 5,000 people died. Near the city of Rasht, a dam burst, and floods swept more villages away.

An Iranian mother comforts her young son after the 1990 earthquake. The apartment block in which they lived was one of thousands wrecked by the quake.

EYEWITNESS

In the village of Hir, 71-year-old Baba Kamalyari was taking a walk to cure sleeplessness when the quake struck, triggering a landslide. 'I saw how the earth was trembling, like nature kicking a cradle. I saw the mountain slide toward the village and said: "God is great! I am ready to die".' Kamalyari watched in horror as a huge boulder crushed his home. He was one of just eight survivors from a village of 1,000.

Survivors of the 1990 quake reach out to catch emergency supplies delivered by truck.

Survivors in the rubble

Rescue services were summoned. Soldiers, rescuers and ordinary people pulled dust-caked victims from the rubble. Red Crescent medical staff tended the injured, while soldiers began the grim work of burying the dead. French rescue teams arrived within a day, with dogs trained to sniff out survivors. However, three days later severe aftershocks rocked the region, claiming more lives. The earthquake was the deadliest ever recorded in Iran, which has a long history of violent quakes.

AT-A-GLANCE

Time and location: 21 June 1990; Gilan and Zanjan Provinces, north-west Iran

Magnitude: 7.4, with 6.5 aftershock

Victims: Around 35,000 killed, 60,000 injured; around 750,000 people left homeless

Worst affected cities: Rudbar, Manjil, Astara, Zanjan and Lushan

Estimated damage: Over US$1 billion

Kobe, 1995

On 17 January 1995 an earthquake conference was planned in south-western Japan. Experts were due to discuss whether the region was prepared for an earthquake. The conference was cancelled because a major quake struck the port of Kobe that very morning. Events showed the region was poorly prepared.

Violent wake-up

The quake hit at 5.46 am, when most of Kobe was sleeping. People were woken by a deep rumble and the crash of masonry and glass. Thousands of older buildings collapsed. The Hanshin Expressway, which snaked through the city on tall pillars, came crashing to the ground. Hundreds of fires were sparked by broken electricity and gas lines. Wooden buildings burned fiercely.

The Kobe earthquake wrecked this section of the Hanshin Expressway. The quake was the largest to hit Japan since 1923.

SAVING LIVES

Many fires raged unchecked in Kobe because streets blocked with traffic and debris prevented fire crews getting through. Worse still, water supplies ran low because of broken water pipes. Some fire teams managed to pump water from the harbour to douse the flames.

Search and rescue

Faint cries of survivors rose from the ruins. SAR teams and 30,000 troops rushed to the scene. They fought fires and shifted rubble to free victims. Injuries were treated. Over 20,000 homeless were taken to emergency shelters such as schools. In all, 6,300 people died in the disaster. The death toll would have been higher had the quake struck a little later, when people would have been on their way to work or school.

Japanese troops search for missing people in the ruins of Kobe. The port area was most badly affected because the quake struck 20 kilometres off the coast.

ONE YEAR ON

Kobe recovered fairly quickly from the disaster. The quake left a million homes without gas, electricity, water or telephone lines. Electricity and telecommunications were repaired within a month. Water and gas took longer. The rail network was badly damaged, but 80 per cent of services were restored in a month. The port reopened a year later.

Indonesian Earthquake and Tsunami, 2004

On the Indonesian island of Sumatra, 26 December 2004 dawned clear and calm. Swimmers and surfers were taking an early dip on the coast of Aceh Province. Just before 8 am, a massive earthquake shook the seabed offshore. People screamed as seafront buildings collapsed, but worse was to follow.

Giant waves

About 15 minutes after the quake, water drained away from the shore. Few people knew this was a sign that giant waves called tsunamis were about to strike. Soon a wall of water appeared on the horizon. It crashed ashore, snapping off palm trees like matchsticks. Cars and people were swept away.

This view from a plane shows the devastation caused by tsunamis to the coast of Banda Aceh. Floodwaters lingered for days.

BREAKING NEWS

26 December 2004, 9 am, Sumatra ...

A very powerful earthquake, rated 9.1, has rocked the bed of the Indian Ocean. Experts believe the quake struck in a deep trench offshore, where tectonic plates are colliding. The quake shifted a huge mass of water. This triggered tsunamis that have wrecked towns along the Sumatran coast.

Destruction of a city

The roaring water swept far inland, wrecking much of Aceh Province. The main city, Banda Aceh, was utterly flattened, as if hit by an atomic bomb. Survivors who managed to reach higher ground returned to the wreckage. They waded into the water to rescue victims, but many people had drowned.

A man stands in the ruins of his home in Banda Aceh. Few private homes survived the tsunamis, but some public buildings, such as churches, stood up better to the battering waves.

RESCUE!

Rizal Shaputra was cleaning a mosque on the coast when the tsunamis struck. He was swept out to sea with several fellow workers. Rizal clambered onto a raft of floating vegetation. 'At first there were some friends with me. After a few days they were gone…. I saw bodies left and right.' He survived by drinking rainwater and eating coconuts attached to the palm trees on his raft. After nine days a container ship picked him up 160 kilometres from shore.

Indian Ocean Tsunami, 2004

Sumatra was not the only place to suffer from the Indonesian earthquake. Tsunamis spread right across the ocean like ripples in a pond. Out to sea, low waves raced across the ocean. Close to shore, they reared to heights of 15 metres and then smashed onto the coast.

Battered coastlines

On the shores of the Indian Ocean, people had no way of knowing that disaster was approaching. One and a half hours after the quake, tsunamis reached the coast of Thailand. Hotels took a pounding. Fishing boats were tossed inland. After two hours, waves hammered Sri Lanka, off southern India. An eyewitness saw 'a wall, like a cliff-face of water, coming straight for us'. The waves washed a train off its tracks. After seven hours they pummelled the African coast.

Terrible toll

The scale of the destruction was enormous. Around 283,000 people died, and over a million were made homeless. Governments around the world sent rescue teams, medical staff and supplies. Hundreds of emergency camps were set up. Clean water was a top priority. In Thailand and India, elephants and bulldozers cleared the debris, so rebuilding could begin.

SAVING LIVES

Ten-year old schoolgirl Tilly Smith was on holiday in Thailand when the tsunamis struck. Water drained away from the beach where she was playing. Remembering a geography lesson about tsunamis, she shouted a warning. Everyone fled. Tilly's prompt action saved many lives.

This resort on the coast of Thailand was wrecked by the tsunamis. Tourism is a major industry in Thailand. Rebuilding tourist accommodation was a priority, so visitors could return, bringing in cash.

TWO YEARS ON

The Pacific Ocean has a tsunami warning system. Sensors out in the ocean detect undersea quakes and unusually large waves. The warning is relayed to the coast where loudspeakers warn everyone to head inland. This can save many lives. Two years after the Indonesian quake a similar system was set up in the Indian Ocean.

Kashmir, 2005

On 8 October 2005 a severe earthquake brought death and disaster to a region already troubled by conflict. The quake struck Kashmir, high in the Himalayas, on an autumn morning in the month of Ramadan. At this time Muslims do not eat between dawn and dusk. At 8.50 am many people were indoors, snoozing after a pre-dawn meal. Children were in school.

BREAKING NEWS

8 October 2005, Kashmir ...
A violent earthquake measuring 7.6 has struck the remote state of Kashmir, which is claimed by both India and Pakistan. The quake struck close to Muzaffarabad, in the zone controlled by Pakistan. The Pakistan capital, Islamabad, 100 kilometres away, was badly damaged.

An Indian woman in the ruins of her home in Indian Kashmir. Thousands of buildings in both India and Pakistan were destroyed.

Buried villages

The quake set off hundreds of landslides. Rockfalls filled gorges, and rivers changed course. Many roads were blocked, including the Karakorum Highway, the main route to this remote region. Whole villages were buried and many schools collapsed. In one village, 49 out of 50 victims were children. Weeping survivors dug for loved ones in the ruins. The disaster claimed 74,500 victims, with 106,000 injured.

Helping the survivors

Over the next few weeks, more than a thousand aftershocks hit the region. Landslides and bad weather prevented rescuers from reaching mountain villages. Soon the winter snows would arrive, closing more roads. The government appealed to survivors to come to the valleys to seek shelter. Soon long lines of ragged survivors were streaming into rescue centres. Nearly 4 million people huddled in 'tent cities' in sub-zero temperatures. Many countries sent medical teams, food and supplies.

SAVING LIVES

India and Pakistan have come close to war over rival claims to Kashmir. In 2005 the two nations made a special truce so that aid could reach the stricken region. Five crossing points were opened along the usually closed border to allow supplies and SAR teams through.

A Turkish SAR team tend a survivor whom they have pulled from a ruined building in Muzaffarabad. The Turkish team arrived just 24 hours after the quake.

China, 2008

In Sichuan Province, western China, 12 May 2008 was an ordinary school and working day. At Juyuan Middle School, Dujiangyan, pupils were hard at work when a massive earthquake struck. The shock waves were felt throughout China.

School collapse

The quake hit at 2.28 pm when older pupils were in lessons. Young children were taking a nap. The three-storey Middle School collapsed, trapping 900 staff and pupils. Survivors who had escaped outside clung to one another, sobbing. Meanwhile frantic parents rushed to the school and began clawing at the rubble with bare hands.

Students at Juyuan Middle School care for an injured boy whose leg has been trapped in the debris caused by the 2008 quake.

EYEWITNESS

An 11-year-old schoolgirl described the moment the earthquake struck. 'All the students rushed into the playground. Half of our school buildings collapsed. Most of my classmates got away but some were injured. A few teachers were buried.'

Wider catastrophe

Elsewhere in mountainous Sichuan, the quake set off hundreds of landslides. Whole villages were wiped out. In cities, apartment blocks and factories crumbled. Over 70,000 people died and 300,000 were injured. Many victims were children.

Coordinated efforts

Rescuers and troops reached Dujiangyan within two hours. For days, Juyuan Middle School resembled a military operation. Bulldozers cleared the wreckage while troops combed the ruins. Ambulances, with sirens wailing, whisked away the injured. A mobile kitchen gave out food. An international aid organization, Save the Children, set up special children's camps. New teachers were trained to continue pupils' education even without a school.

SIX MONTHS ON

Juyuan Middle School was one of hundreds wrecked by the quake. Angry parents protested to the government that schools had been built to poor building standards. Six months on, a government report confirmed that many schools had been unsafe.

Survivors rest at a refugee camp holding over 20,000 people. Disease is a major risk in overcrowded conditions such as these.

Haiti, 2010

On 12 January 2010, disaster struck the Caribbean state of Haiti. Located on the island of Hispaniola, Haiti is one of the world's poorest countries. The island is regularly hit by destructive hurricanes. Now a violent earthquake had occurred.

Devastated capital

The quake hit just before 5 pm, at the end of a working day. The capital, Port-au-Prince, became a sea of rubble. The presidential palace, schools and hospitals lay in ruins. Thousands of badly built homes collapsed, burying people alive. Nearby towns and cities suffered the same fate.

Survivors of the Haiti earthquake make their way through streets littered with debris in the capital, Port-au-Prince.

BREAKING NEWS

12 January 2010, Haiti …

A powerful quake measuring 7.0 has hit Haiti. The epicentre was about 20 kilometres south-west of the capital. The country lies on a major faultline where tectonic plates scrape past one another. The first quake was followed by two aftershocks, both over 5.5 magnitude. Thousands are feared dead.

Isolated country

SAR teams across the world went on alert. But with roads, bridges, the airport and main port out of action, Haiti was largely cut off from the outside world. Cries of victims rose from the rubble. Police and weeping survivors dug with spades, pickaxes and anything to hand. The city morgue was soon overflowing. Bodies were buried in mass graves. The stench of death filled the air. People spent the night outside because of the risk of further collapse.

Slow progress

By 16 January, four days after the quake, a major rescue operation was under way. The airport had been hastily repaired and the first rescue teams had flown in. However, recovery was slow. Six months on, 1.6 million were still in emergency camps. Little of the rubble had been cleared, and thousands of bodies were still unburied. Experts said it would take Haiti ten years to recover from the disaster.

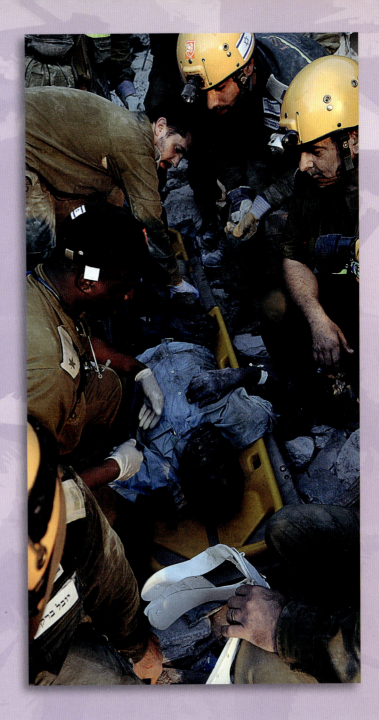

An Israeli SAR team pull a survivor from the rubble five days after the quake. It took eight hours to dig him out.

EYEWITNESS

A US official was in Haiti when the ground started shaking. 'I just held on and bounced across the wall. I heard a tremendous noise and shouting and screaming in the distance. Everybody was totally freaked out and shaken.'

Japanese Tsunami, 2011

On 11 March 2011, a massive undersea earthquake occurred off the coast of Japan. The quake triggered a series of highly destructive tsunamis that hit Japan minutes later.

Earth mover

The earthquake measured 9.0 on the Richter Scale and was the most powerful to hit Japan since records began. The island of Honshu actually moved 2.4 metres to the east and the Earth was shifted on its axis by almost 10 centimetres. The tsunamis that followed were felt along the Pacific coasts of North and South America, including Chile, 17,000 kilometres from Japan.

A tsunami engulfs a residential area in Natori, north-eastern Japan, on 11 March. The city of 74,000 people was virtually destroyed by the waves.

RESCUE!

Risking fires and aftershocks, a rescue team returned to the devastated city of Kesennuma three days after the quake. They heard faint cries of help from beneath the rubble. After hours of careful excavation, they managed to rescue an elderly couple who had been trapped in their collapsed house.

The city of Kamaishi in Iwate, Japan, was protected by a deep tsunami protection breakwater. Yet waves up to 4.3 metres high surmounted the breakwater and flooded the city.

Terrible destruction

The tsunami waves that hit the Japanese coast travelled up to 10 kilometres inland. They swept away cars, bridges, trains and even buildings. In some cases, whole towns were wiped off the map. Hundreds of thousands were made homeless by the disaster and millions were left without water and electricity, due to damage to power stations. One wave damaged a nuclear power plant, causing a serious radiation leak.

AT-A-GLANCE

Time and location: 11 March 2011, 2.46 pm; Tohoku region, north-eastern Japan

Magnitude: 9.0, with over 600 aftershocks measuring 4.5 and above

Victims: 10,000 killed, 3,000 injured, 16,500 missing (by 25 March 2011)

Worst affected cities: Kuji, Ofunato, Rikuzentakata, Kamiashi, Miyako, Ostuchi

Estimated damage: US$309 billion

Preparing for Earthquakes

Earthquakes are an incredibly powerful force of nature. No one can prevent them, but scientists can now pinpoint areas that are most at risk. Careful planning and preparation can reduce the number of deaths caused by quakes.

Scientists now know a lot more about earthquakes than people did a century ago, when a quake wrecked San Francisco. We know that quakes are caused by plate movement, and often strike along plate edges. In quake-prone regions, instruments monitor rocks shifting underground. If experts believe a quake is likely, the emergency services are alerted. Cities can be evacuated. Prompt action can save thousands of lives.

A scientist from Taiwan compares computer readings of two earthquakes that struck Taiwan in a single day. The printout shows vibrations – the shaking caused by the quakes.

Cities can be designed with earthquakes in mind. Engineers assess the risk of fire, floods and landslides. Wide streets reduce the risk from falling buildings. Strong tanks hold water to fight fires. Houses can be built with deep foundations and flexible frames, designed to sway rather than topple. Unstable ground can be avoided. All these measures can reduce death and injury in the event of a quake.

SAVING LIVES

In Japan, San Francisco and other quake-prone areas, earthquake drills are held in schools and workplaces. Children and adults are taught to shelter in a doorway or under a table if the ground shakes. Emergency services practise rescues so they are ready for a crisis.

EIGHTEEN YEARS ON

With its soft soil, Mexico City is at great risk of earthquakes. High-rise buildings are especially under threat. Yet one of the world's tallest buildings rose here in 2003, 18 years after the devastating quake. The Torre Mayor has 96 shock absorbers to cope with vibrations. The design works so well that when a quake hit in 2003, no one inside realized it had struck.

School children from the Philippines use books to protect their heads during an earthquake drill. Sheltering under desks or in doorways may also help to save lives.

Glossary

aftershock A minor earthquake that follows a serious quake.

avalanche A mass of snow that slides down a mountain.

death toll The number of people who die, for example, in a natural disaster.

detection equipment Equipment used to locate something or someone.

earthquake When the ground shakes as rocks shift underground.

epicentre The point on the Earth's surface that lies directly above the focus of an earthquake.

evacuation When everyone is ordered to leave an area.

faultline A deep crack in rocks, often located near the borders of tectonic plates. Earthquakes commonly occur along faultlines, which are also known as faults.

focus The point deep underground where rocks shatter in an earthquake.

heat-sensing equipment Special cameras that can detect warm spots under rubble, which might be the body heat of surviving victims.

incubator A life-support machine for a newborn baby.

landslide A mass of rock and soil that slides downhill.

magnitude The size and strength of an earthquake.

monitor To keep a check on something.

morgue A building where dead bodies are kept before burial or cremation.

radiation Energy emitted in the form of particles by substances such as uranium and plutonium. In large quantities, radiation damages living things.

Richter Scale A system for rating the strength of earthquakes by measuring shock waves.

rubble Rough fragments of stone, brick, concrete and other materials, which form the debris of collapsed buildings.

SAR teams Search and rescue teams are emergency teams that detect and rescue people following disasters such as earthquakes.

shock waves Vibrations caused by earthquakes that pass through the ground. Shock waves are also called seismic waves.

sniffer dogs Dogs that have been trained to use their sense of smell to locate earthquake victims buried under rubble.

tectonic plate One of the huge, rigid plates that make up the Earth's outer layer. Tectonic plates are in slow but constant motion.

tsunami A giant wave or series of waves set off by an undersea earthquake.

vibration The act of vibrating, or moving quickly to and fro.

Further Information

Books
Amazing Planet Earth: Earthquakes and Tsunamis by Terry Jennings (Franklin Watts, 2009)
DK Eyewitness Guide: Natural Disasters by Clare Watts (Dorling Kindersley, 2006)
Natural Disasters: Earthquakes by Ewan McLeish (Wayland, 2010)
Nature's Fury: Earthquake by Anne Rooney (Franklin Watts, 2006)
Real Life Heroes: Stories about Surviving Natural Disasters by Jen Green (Franklin Watts, 2010)

Websites
www.earthquakes.com
   The Global Earthquake Response Center

earthquake.usgs.gov/regional/neic
   The National Earthquake Information Center – a US government website

www.eri.u-tokyo.ac.jp/eng
   The Earthquake Research Institute, University of Tokyo

news.bbc.co.uk/1/hi/4126809.stm
   A BBC site about earthquakes and why they happen

tsunami.geo.ed.ac.uk/local-bin/quakes/mapscript/home.pl
   The World-Wide Earthquake Locator

Index

Page numbers in **bold** refer to pictures.

aftershocks 5, 10, 13, 21, 24, 26, 30
aid 6, 7, **13**, 18, 21, 23
Armenia (1988), earthquake in 4
avalanches 5, 30

Banda Aceh **16**, 17, **17**

Chile (2010), earthquake in 6

dams 5, 13
disease 7

earthquake drills 29, **29**
earthquake-resistant buildings 29
emergency services 6, 28, 29
epicenter 24, 30
evacuation 28, 30

fault lines 4, 8, 10, 24, 30
firefighters 6, 9, 14, 15
fires 5, **5**, 6, 9, 14, 15, 29
floods 5, **5**, 12, 16, **16**, 17, **27**, 29
focus 4, 30

Haiti (2010), earthquake in 7, **7**, 24–25, **24**, **25**

Indian Ocean earthquake and tsunami (2004) 16–19, **16**, **17**, **19**
Iran (1990), earthquake in 12–13, **12**, **13**

Japan (2011), earthquake and tsunami in 26–27, **26**, **27**

Kashmir (2005), earthquake in 20–21, **20**, **21**
Kobe, Japan (1995), earthquake in 14–15, **14**, **15**

landslides 5, 10, 12, 20, 21, 23, 29, 30
Los Angeles (1994), earthquake in 5

medical teams 13, 18, 21
medical treatment 6, **7**, 13, 15
Mexico City (1985), earthquake in 10–11, **11**, 29

Port-au-Prince, Haiti 24, **24**
preparing for earthquakes 28–29

reconstruction 7, 9, 15, 18
rescuers 5, 7, 10, 13, 17, 18, 21, 23, 25, 26
Richter Scale 5, 16, 20, 24, 26, 27, 30

rubble, clearing 6, 7, 10, 11, 13, 15, **15**, 18, 25, 26

San Francisco (1906), earthquake in 8–9, **8**, **9**, 28
search and rescue (SAR) teams 6, 15, **15**, 21, **21**, 25, **25**, 26
shelter, temporary 7, 9, **9**, 15, 18, 21, **23**
shock waves 4, 10, 22, 30
Sichuan Province, China (2008), earthquake in 22–23, **22**, **23**
sniffer dogs 6, **6**, 10, 13
Sri Lanka 18

tectonic plates 4, 10, 16, 24, 28, 30
Thailand 18, **19**
tsunamis 5, 16, **16**, 17, 18, 27–27, **26**, **27**, 30
tsunami warning systems 19

undersea earthquakes 5, 10, 16, 26

water supplies 7, 9, 15, 18, 27